I0448785

Informing the legislative debate since 1914 _____

Guam: U.S. Defense Deployments

Shirley A. Kan
Specialist in Asian Security Affairs

June 9, 2014

Congressional Research Service

7-5700

www.crs.gov

RS22570

Summary

Since 2000, the U.S. military has been building up forward-deployed forces on the westernmost U.S. territory of Guam (west of Hawaii) to increase U.S. operational presence, deterrence, and power projection for potential responses to crises, disasters, or other contingencies to support Japan, Republic of Korea (ROK), the Philippines, Taiwan, or others in Asia. Since 2006, joint exercises based at Guam called "Valiant Shield" have boosted U.S. military readiness in the Pacific. The defense buildup on Guam has been moderate. China has concerns, suspecting Guam's buildup to be directed against China. There has been concern that China and North Korea could target Guam with missiles. China's People's Liberation Army (PLA) Navy has increased activities in waters around Guam. Still, Guam's role expanded in engaging with the PLA.

In 2006, the United States and Japan had agreed on a Realignment Roadmap to strengthen their alliance, including a buildup on Guam to cost $10.3 billion, with Japan contributing 60%. Goals were to start the related construction on Guam by 2010 and to complete relocation of about 8,000 marines from Okinawa to Guam by 2014. In Tokyo on February 17, 2009, the Secretary of State signed a U.S.-Japan agreement on the relocation of the III Marine Expeditionary Force personnel from Okinawa to Guam that reaffirmed the "Roadmap" of May 1, 2006. However, the marines' relocation will not occur by 2014 and will be more geographically distributed. Opposition on Okinawa to the U.S.-Japan plan for a Futenma Replacement Facility (FRF) to replace the Marine Corps Air Station Futenma brought implications for the marines' move from Okinawa to Guam. Despite the dispute over the FRF, Japan has budgeted for its contributions to the marines' move.

By 2011, some Members urged attention to concerns that included Japan's impasse, expanded costs, and the delay in the realignment even as a strong U.S. military presence and readiness remain critical in the Asia-Pacific. On May 11, 2011, Senators Carl Levin, John McCain, and Jim Webb called for a review of plans to restructure military forces in Japan, ROK, and Guam, in order to make progress. President Obama issued in January 2012 the defense guidance for the strategy of "rebalancing" diplomatic, defense, and economic priorities more to the Asia-Pacific. This "rebalance" further raised Guam's profile as a "strategic hub." Finally, on February 8, the United States and Japan agreed to "adjust" the Roadmap and separate the move of marines from the plan for the FRF, in order to make progress separately. A U.S.-Japan Joint Statement of April 2012 specified that out of about 9,000 marines to be relocated from Okinawa, about 5,000 marines would move to Guam. Out of the new estimated cost of $8.6 billion, Japan would contribute $3.1 billion. A U.S.-Japan Joint Statement of October 2013 pointed to a later relocation of marines to Guam that will start in the first half of the 2020s. Before construction, preparation includes a draft environmental study (issued in April 2014), final study (2015), and master plan.

After China announced an "East China Sea Air Defense Identification Zone (ADIZ)" in November 2013, the U.S. Air Force flew two B-52 bombers from Guam into the ADIZ in defiance of China's rules for notification. In April 2014, President Obama issued a U.S.-Japan Joint Statement, reaffirming that "the United States and Japan are also making sustained progress towards realizing a geographically distributed, operationally resilient, and politically sustainable U.S. force posture in the Asia Pacific, including the development of Guam as a strategic hub."

Legislation includes the National Defense Authorization Act (NDAA) for FY2014, **P.L. 113-66**, which authorized a total of $494,607,000 for projects on Guam; **H.R. 4495** (Forbes); and FY2015 NDAA, **H.R. 4435** (McKeon) and **S. 2410** (Levin). Updated as warranted, this CRS Report discusses major developments and policy issues related to the defense buildup.

Contents

Strategic Significance of Guam for Defense Buildup 1

Force Relocations and Deployments from the U.S. Mainland 2

U.S. Force Relocations from Japan 3

    Agreement 4

    Budgets 7

Concerns and Issues for Congress 7

    Rationales 7

    Concerns 9

    Allies and Partners 17

    China 19

    Major Legislation 25

Tables

Table 1. Illustrative Sailing Distances and Time 8

Contacts

Author Contact Information 28

Strategic Significance of Guam for Defense Buildup

Guam is the westernmost U.S. territory long valued as strategically significant to U.S. forward deployments in the Western Pacific. Historically, the United States acquired Guam from Spain in 1898 after the Spanish-American War. In the Pacific Ocean, Hawaii is about 2,400 miles west of California, and Guam is about 3,800 miles further west of Hawaii. Guam has two important U.S. military bases: Apra Naval Base and Andersen Air Force Base. The island, three times the size of Washington, DC, is home to about 160,000 people. There are about 6,000 military personnel. As the Defense Department faced increased tension on the Korean peninsula, the Pacific Command (PACOM) began in 2000 to build up air and naval forces on Guam to boost U.S. deterrence and power projection in Asia. Concerns include crisis response, counterterrorism, and contingencies in the Pacific. The defense buildup on Guam has been moderate.

Guam is critical to enhancing the forward presence, strengthening alliances, and shaping China's rise. Visiting Guam in May 2008, Defense Secretary Robert Gates said that Guam's buildup will be "one of the largest movements of military assets in decades" and will help to "maintain a robust military presence in a critical part of the world."[1] Under President Obama, Secretary Gates issued the Quadrennial Defense Review (QDR) in February 2010, in which the United States noted the importance of implementing the U.S.-Japan Realignment Roadmap of 2006 that will ensure the deployment of U.S. forces in Japan and transform Guam into a regional security hub. The QDR also announced the development of a new joint Air-Sea Battle Concept, to integrate the air, sea, land, space, and cyberspace forces of the Air Force and Navy to counter challenges to U.S. freedom of action, defeat adversaries with sophisticated anti-access and area-denial (A2/AD) capabilities, and improve power projection operations.

As part of the Obama Administration's effort to re-engage throughout the Asian-Pacific region and reassure allies and partners facing a rising China that views the United States as an "outside" power, Gates participated at an annual Asian-Pacific defense ministers' meeting in June 2010 in Singapore at which he declared that the United States is a Pacific nation and will remain a "power in the Pacific." He highlighted the South China Sea as an area of growing concern. He also stated that the defense buildup on Guam is part of a shift in the U.S. defense posture in Asia, a shift to be more geographically distributed, operationally resilient, and politically sustainable. Deputy Defense Secretary William Lynn III visited Guam in July and stressed Guam's value, saying "from bases here, our forces can ensure the security of our allies, quickly respond to disaster and humanitarian needs, safeguard the sea lanes that are so vital to the world economy, and address any military provocation that may occur." The Chairman of the Joint Chiefs of Staff issued strategic guidance for 2011 that placed priority on U.S. security interests in the Middle East, Afghanistan, and Pakistan. Still, he declared a sharper focus on the Asian-Pacific region in balancing risks from an aggressive North Korea and a more assertive China and in defending freedom of navigation. With the U.S. military's drawdown from Afghanistan and Iraq, the U.S. defense strategy of January 2012 declared a "rebalancing" toward a strengthened presence in the Pacific. In May 2014, Defense Secretary Chuck Hagel said that the Deputy Secretary of Defense will oversee the enhancement of the U.S. force posture in Japan, South Korea, and Guam.[2]

---

[1] Donna Miles, "Gates Views Growth Under Way in Guam," *American Forces Press Service*, May 30, 2008.

[2] Secretary of Defense Robert Gates, speech at Shangri-La Dialogue (meeting of defense ministers), Singapore, June 5, 2010; Deputy Secretary of Defense William Lynn III, Remarks at the University of Guam, July 27, 2010; Secretary of Defense Chuck Hagel, speech at Shangri-La Dialogue, Singapore, May 31, 2014.

Force Relocations and Deployments from the U.S. Mainland

Guam's strategic significance has risen steadily. In 2000, the Air Force reportedly sought to base elements of an Air Expeditionary Force in Guam and sent B-2 stealth bombers to Guam to expand the range of U.S. options for contingencies involving North Korea. As PACOM's Commander, Admiral Dennis Blair acquired approval to forward deploy air-launched cruise missiles on Guam for the first time in August 2000. The Air Force moved precision munitions to be stockpiled on Guam, including Joint Direct Attack Munitions and Joint Standoff Weapons.[3]

In February 1997, Guam's Delegate Robert Underwood noted in the House that an aircraft carrier (USS *Independence*, homeported in Japan) visited Guam for the first time in more than 30 years. In early 2001, the Navy announced that it would station up to three nuclear-power attack submarines (SSNs) at Guam, in order to shorten the transit time compared to travel from homeports in Hawaii or California to the western Pacific and to shorten deployments for sailors. The first submarine to be based at Guam arrived in 2002. In 2007, the USS *Buffalo* joined USS *Houston* and USS *City of Corpus Christi* as the three SSNs based at Guam. (Since then, different SSNs have replaced those first SSNs with their homeports in Guam.) The Quadrennial Defense Review (QDR) of 2006 called for an adjustment in U.S. force posture, with a greater presence in the Pacific than that in the Atlantic (including at least six aircraft carriers and 60% of submarines in the Pacific). In 2007, the Navy decided not to homeport the aircraft carrier USS *Carl Vinson* at Guam. Nonetheless, by 2008, the Navy planned for a transient berth in Apra Harbor to support an aircraft carrier for up to three times a year, each visit for up to three weeks. The QDR of 2010 called for maintaining a force structure of 10-11 aircraft carriers. In mid-2010, three Ohio-class guided-missile submarines (SSGNs), USS *Michigan*, USS *Ohio*, and USS *Florida*, showed their presence in the Pacific and used Guam to support their operations. In June 2012, five Los Angeles-class SSNs and one Ohio-class SSGN simultaneously converged at Guam, in part for repairs and maintenance.[4] In June 2012, Defense Secretary Leon Panetta provided some details for the strategic "rebalance" to the Asia-Pacific, saying that, by 2020, 60% of the Navy's fleets would be in the Pacific, including 6 of 11 aircraft carriers. On April 8, 2013, Deputy Secretary of Defense Ashton Carter announced that the Navy will deploy a fourth SSN to Guam by 2015. The Navy announced in February 2014 that the USS *Topeka* will be that SSN. Guam's three SSNs form part of the force of 56% of the total SSNs that are deployed to the Pacific, as of end of 2013.

In 2002, the Commander of Pacific Air Forces publicly detailed his request for basing aircraft in Guam. In addition to munitions stockpiles and jet fuel, he reportedly requested F-22 stealth fighters, 767 tankers, C-17 transports, bombers, and Global Hawk reconnaissance drones.[5] In

---

[3] Thomas Ricks, "For Pentagon, Asia Moving to Forefront," *Washington Post*, May 26, 2000; "Inside the Ring," *Washington Times*, August 25, 2000; Robert Burns, "Air Force Plan Could Place Bombers Closer to Targets," *Seattle Times*, November 30, 2000.

[4] U.S. House of Representatives, "A Fair Hearing on Guam," *Congressional Record*, February 25, 1997; Christian Bohmfalk, "Navy Decides to Homeport Up to Three Attack Submarines in Guam," *Inside the Navy*, January 29, 2001; Nathan Hodge, "Navy Basing Subs in Guam," *Defense Week*, October 1, 2002; Nelson Daranciang, "Senators Hope Naval Presence Will Grow," *Honolulu Star-Bulletin*, March 31, 2007; *Navy Newsstand*, July 12, 2007; Navy Secretary Donald Winter, "Report on Department of Defense Planning Efforts for Guam," September 15, 2008; Commander, Submarine Force, U.S. Pacific Fleet, December 4, 2009; *South China Morning Post*, July 4, 2010; "Guam Welcomes Submarines," *Navy News Service*, June 8, 2012.

[5] Jim Wolf, "U.S. General Urges Warplanes Be Sent to Guam," *Reuters*, August 23, 2002.

March 2003, after a new Air Expeditionary Wing was activated at Guam's Andersen Air Force Base, B-1 and B-52 bombers deployed temporarily on a rotational basis from air bases in Texas and Louisiana as U.S. forces prepared for war against Iraq. Beyond rotation of aircraft, the Air Force began continuous deployment of aircraft into Guam. As part of this buildup, the first B-52 bombers (stationed out of Minot Air Force Base in North Dakota) to deploy to Andersen arrived in February 2004. B-52 bombers can each carry 20 AGM-86C/D conventional air-launched cruise missiles (CALCMs), and these long-range weapons have been fielded at Andersen.[6] In April 2005, the Commander of Pacific Air Forces said that B-2 stealth bombers started to fly out of Andersen. In April 2005, F-15 fighters temporarily deployed to Andersen from Idaho. An Air Force official said in 2006 that the Air Force planned to station KC-135 tankers on Guam. In May 2007, the Air Force announced the deployment of 18 F-16 fighters to Guam for four months. In the summer of 2008, several F-22 fighters, based in Alaska since 2007, began deployments to Guam. Also, Andersen Air Force Base first planned to have four to six RQ-4 Global Hawk unmanned aerial vehicles (UAVs) for an Intelligence, Surveillance, and Reconnaissance (ISR) Strike Task Force by 2009, but the first of three RQ-4 Global Hawks arrived in September 2010. Andersen also plans to host the MQ-4C Broad Area Maritime Surveillance Triton drones in 2017. The Chief of Naval Operations (CNO), Admiral Jonathan Greenert, explained in November 2012 that the strategic rebalancing of priorities and expansion of air surveillance operations involve the operation of the Navy's MQ-4 Global Hawk UAVs from Guam by the middle of the decade.[7] Facing the Democratic People's Republic of Korea's (DPRK's) announced threats against Guam in March 2013, the Defense Department announced on April 3 that it would deploy to Guam within weeks a Terminal High Altitude Area Defense (THAAD) ballistic missile defense system as a precautionary measure to improve defenses against the DPRK's missile threat.

U.S. Force Relocations from Japan

Originally, the United States and Japan agreed in October 2005 to realign the U.S. force posture, in part to sustain the alliance and meet the needs of the changing security situation. In a "2+2" joint statement, the Secretaries of State and Defense, and their Japanese counterparts, agreed, *inter alia*, to expand the training of Japan's Self-Defense Forces (SDF) in Guam, Alaska, Hawaii, and the U.S. mainland, and to realign U.S. Marine Corps forces for more flexible responses to crises (including by moving about 7,000 marines plus dependents from Okinawa to Guam). In May 2006, the United States and Japan signed a detailed "Roadmap" to implement the realignment, in part by agreeing to move about 8,000 marines of the III Marine Expeditionary

---

[6] PACOM, "B-1Bs, B-52Hs Arrive in Guam," March 6, 2003; Robert Burns, "Air Force Wants to Put Fighters and Bombers Back on Guam in Pacific," *AP*, January 13, 2004; Michael Sirak, "U.S. Considers Bomber Presence on Guam," *Jane's Defense Weekly*, January 21, 2004; PACOM, "Bomber Deployment to Guam," February 2, 2004; "Bombers Arrive At Andersen," *AFN*; Katie Worth, "B-52 Bombers Arrive," *Pacific Daily News*, February 23, 2004; U.S. Air Force, "AGM-86B/C/D Missiles." There is also the AGM-86B version with a nuclear warhead.

[7] Martin Matishak, "Hester: Air Force to Bolster Presence in Asia-Pacific Region," *Inside the Air Force*, April 29, 2005; Natalie Quinata, "Fighter Squadron Arrives on Guam," *Pacific Daily News*, April 30, 2005; Gregg Kakesako, "U.S. Military to Beef Up Its Presence on Guam," *Honolulu Star-Bulletin*, June 21, 2006; "United States to Deploy 18 F-16s to Guam," *Reuters News*, May 24, 2007; Frank Whitman, "No Big Changes at Andersen Right Away, New 36th Wing Commander Says," *Stars and Stripes*, November 18, 2006; Audrey McAvoy, "Air Force to Deploy Alaska-Based F-22 Raptors to Guam," *AP*, May 21, 2008, quoting the Commander of Pacific Air Forces, General Carrol Chandler; "Rear Admiral Addresses Business Leaders on Guam's Military Importance," *KUAM*, February 25, 2009; Travis Tritten, "Andersen Receives Pacific's First Global Hawk Drone," *Stars and Stripes*, September 8, 2010; "USAF Welcomes RQ-4 Global Hawk to Guam Watch," *Flight International*, September 28-October 4, 2010; *Stars and Stripes*, August 17, 2012; Jonathan Greenert, "The Navy Pivots to Asia," *Foreign Policy*, November 14, 2012.

Force (MEF) and about 9,000 dependents from Okinawa to Guam by 2014. The relocation was estimated to cost $10.27 billion. Of this amount, Japan pledged to provide $6.09 billion (including $2.8 billion in direct contribution to develop Guam's facilities and infrastructure).[8]

Agreement

On February 5, 2009, Admiral Timothy Keating, Commander of the Pacific Command (PACOM), told *Reuters* that the transfer of 8,000 marines to Guam might be delayed and cost more, but observers questioned his authority for the statement. Indeed, PACOM clarified the next day that the goals remained to start the related construction by 2010 and to complete relocation by 2014.

III Marine Expeditionary Force (MEF). Soon after, on February 17, 2009, Secretary of State Hillary Clinton visited Tokyo and signed the bilateral "Agreement Between the Government of the United States of America and the Government of Japan Concerning the Implementation of the Relocation of the III Marine Expeditionary Force Personnel and Their Dependents From Okinawa to Guam" that reaffirmed the "Roadmap" of May 1, 2006. The two governments agreed that of the estimated $10.27 billion cost of the facilities and infrastructure development for the relocation, Japan would provide $6.09 billion, including up to $2.8 billion in direct cash contributions (in FY2008 dollars). The United States committed to fund $3.18 billion plus about $1 billion for a road for a total of $4.18 billion. Under the agreement, about 8,000 personnel from the III MEF and about 9,000 of their dependents would relocate from Okinawa to Guam by 2014.

Futenma Replacement Facility (FRF). In addition to Japan's financial contribution, the relocation to Guam would have depended upon Japan's progress in completion of the Futenma Replacement Facility (FRF). In the "Roadmap," the United States and Japan agreed to replace the Marine Corps Air Station (MCAS) Futenma with the FRF constructed using landfill and located in another, less populated area of Okinawa (at Camp Schwab). The original plan expected an interconnected package that involved relocation to the FRF, return of MCAS Futenma, transfer of III MEF personnel to Guam, and consolidation of facilities and return of land on Okinawa.

In April 2009, the lower house of Japan's parliament, the Diet, voted to approve the bilateral agreement, and the Diet ratified it on May 13, 2009. The next day, the Department of State welcomed the Diet's ratification of the agreement and reiterated the U.S. commitment to the completion of the relocation of 8,000 marines to Guam from Okinawa, host to about 25,000 U.S. military personnel and their dependents.

However, on September 16, 2009, Yukio Hatoyama of the Democratic Party of Japan (DPJ) became prime minister. This political change raised uncertainty when Japan sought to re-negotiate the agreement even as the United States sought its implementation. The DPJ had called for the Futenma air station to be relocated outside of Okinawa, with concerns about the impact on the local people and environment. In Tokyo on October 21, Defense Secretary Robert Gates stressed to Japan's Defense Minister Toshimi Kitazawa the importance of implementing the agreement by "moving forward expeditiously on the roadmap as agreed." Gates said at a news conference that "without the [FRF], there will be no relocation to Guam. And without relocation to Guam, there will be no consolidation of forces and return of land in Okinawa." But by the time of President Obama's visit on November 13, 2009, the two leaders could only announce a

---

[8] U.S.-Japan Security Consultative Committee, Joint Statements, October 29, 2005, and May 1, 2006.

"working group" to discuss differences. The U.S. side agreed to discuss the agreement's "implementation," but Japan sought to "review" the agreement. At a meeting in Honolulu on January 12, 2010, Secretary of State Hillary Clinton stressed moving on the implementation of the agreement but also acknowledged that the alliance had lots of other business to conduct. She expressed an expectation of a decision on the FRF by May, after Foreign Minister Katsuya Okada conveyed Hatoyama's promise to decide by that time. Visiting Tokyo on January 15, Senator Daniel Inouye said Hatoyama reiterated this promise to decide by May. (On details about Japan's dispute over Futenma, see CRS Report RL33436, *Japan-U.S. Relations: Issues for Congress*.)

Meanwhile, on May 20, 2010, the ROK announced that an international investigation found that an attack on March 26 by the DPRK sank the ROK's naval ship, *Cheonan*, and killed 46 sailors. President Obama condemned that "act of aggression." The crisis provoked by the DPRK catalyzed Japan's resolution of the dispute over the realignment. Moreover, in April, Japan said that China's People's Liberation Army Navy (PLAN) deployed ships and submarines near Japan's southern islands of Okinawa and Miyakojima and dangerously confronted Japan's surveillance forces, including pointing guns from a PLAN destroyer at Japan's maritime patrol plane and flying a helicopter in close approach to Japan's destroyer in at least two incidents. The next month, China's maritime survey ship approached and chased away Japan's Coast Guard survey ship in the East China Sea, demanding that Japan's ship stop its surveys. While the crisis with the DPRK involved an attack that sank the ROK's ship and killed its sailors, the PLA's aggressiveness did not result in conflict at that time. Nonetheless, later in July, Assistant Secretary of Defense for Asian and Pacific Security Affairs Wallace Gregson testified to Congress that both the actions by North Korea and China (the PLAN's deployment of a Surface Action Group near Okinawa) prompted Japan's recognition of a vital U.S. role in Japan's deterrence.[9]

Joint Statements. On May 28, 2010, in Tokyo, Secretary of Defense Gates and Secretary of State Clinton along with their counterparts in Japan issued a "2+2" Joint Statement of the U.S.-Japan Security Consultative Committee. Thus, Japan reaffirmed its commitment to implement the 2006 Roadmap and 2009 Agreement on relocation of marines from Okinawa to Guam. The following month, Japan's new Prime Minister Naoto Kan affirmed the agreement. However, by July 2010, the U.S. Navy expressed doubts about meeting the original goal of completing the relocation of marines to Guam by 2014,[10] supporting Admiral Keating's assessment in 2009.

Just after retiring as an Assistant Secretary of Defense, Gregson said in April 2011 that about 10,000 marines would remain on Okinawa after the relocation of some marines from Okinawa to Guam. Moreover, he clarified that the change would be a "realignment of the alliance to Guam." Not only will there be a buildup of U.S. forces at Guam, but there would be a new continuous presence of Japan's aviation, ground, and naval forces training there.[11] However, Japan's media reported in March 2012 that marines in Okinawa increased from 18,000 to 21,000 by 2011.[12]

In the "2+2" Joint Statement of June 21, 2011, the United States and Japan rhetorically reaffirmed their commitment to implement "steadily" the realignment as agreed in 2006 and the Joint Statement of May 2010. However, the United States and Japan also conceded that the completion

---

[9] Testimony before a hearing of the House Armed Services Committee, July 27, 2010.

[10] Satoshi Ogawa, "U.S. Government Gives Up on Relocating Marines in Okinawa to Guam by 2014," *Yomiuri*, July 23, 2010.

[11] Yoichi Kato, "Japan-U.S. Alliance Will Grow Stronger From Quake," *Asahi Shimbun*, April 10, 2011.

[12] *Jiji Press*, March 16, 2012.

of the FRF and the relocation of marines from Okinawa to Guam will not meet the target date of 2014. After a new Prime Minister, Yoshihiko Noda, took office on September 2, 2011, Japan indicated it would implement the realignment. According to a press briefing by White House officials, President Obama met with Noda at the U.N. in New York on September 21 and stressed the importance for the alliance of implementing the relocation agreements. Before Defense Secretary Leon Panetta left for a trip to Asia, Senator Webb wrote him on October 19, urging a careful reexamination of alternatives to the agreements given the impasse. He wrote that senior officials and officers of the Defense Department expressed to him and Senator Levin some deep concerns about the affordability and workability of the 2006 Roadmap. Nonetheless, on October 25, Secretary Panetta met with Japan's Defense and Foreign Ministers and said that both countries remained committed to the Roadmap and moving marines to Guam.

The impasse in Japan still continued through 2011, and Japan's environmental impact report on Futenma had to be dropped in the cover of darkness at 4:00 AM on December 28 in Okinawa. In early 2012, visiting Diet Members noted the dispute for some pessimism about the realignment.

Finally, on February 8, 2012, after some Members in Congress urged a review of the realignment in realistic recognition of the persistent impasse (see below on congressional actions in May 2011 on a review of the force structure), Japan's officials visited Washington for meetings with Deputy Assistant Secretaries of Defense and State. The two sides agreed to "adjust" the Realignment Roadmap of 2006 and separate the move of marines from the maintenance of the plan for the FRF, in order to make progress separately. The United States and Japan reaffirmed the need to strengthen the alliance and build Guam as a "strategic hub" with an "operational" Marine Corps presence. However, the U.S.-Japan Joint Statement on Defense Posture did not provide numbers and locations for transfers of marines, a timeline, or any changes in costs. Senator Webb noted that the statement was an acknowledgment that the Roadmap must be adjusted to preserve the strength of the alliance and the stability of the region.

The "2+2" Joint Statement of the Security Consultative Committee of April 26 noted the U.S. strategy of January 2012 to "rebalance" defense priorities to the Asia-Pacific and reaffirmed the decision to adjust the realignment. The joint statement expressed an intent to consult with respective legislatures. Two days prior, Senators Levin, McCain, and Webb sent a letter to Secretary Panetta to stress that any new proposal should be not considered final until it has the support of the Congress. As part of the effort for a deeper and broader U.S.-Japan alliance, the two sides have relocated aviation training to Guam and will develop training areas in Guam and the Commonwealth of Northern Mariana Islands (CNMI) as shared-use facilities. The Joint Statement provided more specific numbers for the relocation of marines: out of about 9,000 marines to be relocated from Okinawa, about 5,000 marines would move to Guam, "when appropriate facilities are available to receive them." About 10,000 would remain on Okinawa. The marines in Guam would form one of four Marine Air-Ground Task Forces (MAGTFs) in the Pacific. Concerning a new agreement on costs, the move of marines to Guam would cost $8.6 billion, with Japan's share to be the direct cash contribution agreed in 2009 and with no longer mention of loans. The updated value of Japan's contribution would be $3.1 billion (including for training ranges), according to Department of State and Defense officials who briefed reporters. At a hearing of the House Armed Services Subcommittee on Readiness on August 1, 2012, Defense Department officials acknowledged that they had no timeline for the distributed laydown but called for starting the move of marines to Guam, partly to shore up political support in Japan in accordance with the Joint Statement and to boost U.S. credibility in the "rebalancing" strategy. Representatives Forbes and Bordallo requested a timeline from the Defense Department.[13]

In December 2012, Shinzo Abe of the Liberal Democratic Party (LDP) became Prime Minister, stressing a stronger alliance with the United States. The PACOM Commander, Admiral Samuel Locklear, estimated the completion of the marines' move to Guam by 2020 and to Hawaii by 2026, in testimony to the House Armed Services Committee on March 5, 2013. On April 5, Defense Secretary Chuck Hagel announced an agreement with Japan on a plan to return areas on Okinawa, after replacement facilities are constructed and a sizeable contingent of marines relocate to Guam and Hawaii. However, the U.S.-Japan Joint Statement of the Security Consultative Committee in October 2013 pointed to a later relocation from Okinawa to Guam that will start in the first half of the 2020s. For his visit to Japan in April 2014, President Obama wrote that "as part of the realignment of our forces in Japan, we're working to close the Futenma facility and relocate to a new facility, consolidate our presence on Okinawa into fewer locations and move many of our forces to Guam and Hawaii.... The realignment of our forces—as part of the broader modernization of our defense posture in the region—will ensure that our alliance stays strong and ready for the future." Obama and Abe issued a U.S.-Japan Joint Statement, which reaffirmed that "the United States and Japan are also making sustained progress towards realizing a geographically distributed, operationally resilient, and politically sustainable U.S. force posture in the Asia Pacific, including the development of Guam as a strategic hub."[14]

Budgets

Despite Japan's dispute over the FRF in Okinawa, Japan has allocated funds in the defense budgets for the marines' relocation and buildup on Guam. Japan allocated as direct contributions $336 million in the 2009 defense budget and $497 million in the 2010 budget. (Japan's fiscal year covers April 1 to March 31.) The conference report for the FY2013 NDAA noted that $725 million was unobligated in the U.S. Treasury. Japan's 2013 defense budget included $7.4 million for the relocation of marines from Okinawa to Guam. Japan's 2014 defense budget included about $13.8 million for projects necessary for the relocation of marines from Okinawa to Guam.

Concerns and Issues for Congress

Rationales

One rationale for the military buildup on Guam is its status as a U.S. territory. Thus, the United States is not required to negotiate with sovereign countries on force deployments or face the risks of losing bases or access. Defense Secretary Donald Rumsfeld visited Guam in November 2003 and expressed support for building up Guam as he considered a new round of base closings.[15] In contrast, the United States had to close Subic Bay Naval Base and Clark Air Force Base in the Philippines in 1992. Foreign countries could restrict the use of U.S. forces based there. U.S.

---

[13] House Armed Services Subcommittee on Readiness, hearing on Pacific Command Force Posture, August 1, 2012.

[14] President Obama, Interview published in *Yomiuri Shimbun*'s *Japan News*, April 23, 2014; White House, "U.S.-Japan Joint Statement," Tokyo, Japan, April 25, 2014.

[15] James Brooke, "Looking for Friendly Overseas Base, Pentagon Finds it Already Has One," *New York Times*, April 7, 2004.

forces based in Guam also do not have to contend with political sensitivities over nuclear powered vessels. Moreover, some countries, including allies, have raised doubts at times about their support for U.S. forces in a possible conflict between the United States and China.

Another rationale is the expansion of options that Guam offers to the evolving U.S. force structure. As Commander of PACOM, Admiral William Fallon expressed his vision for Guam as a staging area from which ships, aircraft, and troops can "surge" to the Asian theater. He stressed "flexibility," saying "we need to have forces ready to react," and "we must have built-in flexibility" to meet emergencies (including disaster relief).[16] In 2004, the Navy held "Summer Pulse 04," its first exercise to increase readiness to "surge" operations in response to a crisis. In June 2006, PACOM held the first "Valiant Shield" exercise that brought three aircraft carriers to waters off Guam. The fourth "Valiant Shield" exercise took place near Guam in September 2012, involving the forward-deployed aircraft carrier USS *George Washington*.

A third rationale is the need to counter what commanders call the "tyranny of distance." PACOM, headquartered in Honolulu, has an area of responsibility that encompasses almost 60% of the world's population, over 50% of the earth's surface, the Pacific and Indian Oceans, 16 time zones, and five of seven U.S. defense treaties. U.S. forces on Guam are much closer to East Asia, where the United States has five alliances with Australia, Japan, South Korea, Thailand, and the Philippines. The United States also has concerns about tension and instability in the East China Sea, South China Sea, and Yellow Sea; terrorism in Southeast and South Asia; humanitarian crises; and sea lines of communication (SLOCs), particularly through the Straits of Malacca. Combat aircraft on Guam can reach Taiwan, Japan, Philippines, or the Korean peninsula in two to five hours.[17] Moreover, **Table 1** presents the shorter sailing distance and time from Guam to Manila in East Asia, as an example, compared to that from Honolulu, Seattle, and San Diego.

Table 1. Illustrative Sailing Distances and Time

To Manila, from:	Statute miles	Days at 20 knots	Days at 30 knots
Guam	1,724	3.1	2.1
Honolulu	5,482	9.9	6.6
Seattle	6,853	12.4	8.3
San Diego	7,595	13.8	9.2

Notes: Sailing distances in statute miles were calculated using nautical miles reported by "Distances Between Ports," 2001, published by the National Imagery and Mapping Agency. Also, 1 nautical mile equals 1.15 statute miles, and 1 knot equals 1.15 mph.

Relatedly, under President Obama, the United States has paid greater attention to Southeast Asia. There is concern about potential instability over disputed islands and China's assertiveness in the South China Sea. In February 2011, the Chairman of the Joint Chiefs of Staff, Admiral Mike Mullen, issued a National Military Strategy, declaring that the U.S. military also must invest new attention and resources in Southeast and South Asia, in addition to the long-standing presence in Northeast Asia. PACOM's Commander, Admiral Robert Willard, testified to the House Armed Services Committee in April 2011, elaborating that it has become increasingly important for U.S. forces to attain more access to and support from allies and partners in South and Southeast Asia.

---

[16] Richard Halloran, "Guam Seen as Pivotal U.S. Base," *Washington Times*, March 11, 2006.

[17] Donna Miles, "Gates Views Massive Growth Under Way in Guam," *AFPS*, May 30, 2008.

Concerns

Infrastructure. As U.S. forces relocate to Guam, the state of its infrastructure has been of concern to some policy makers. Also, Guam's political leaders have expressed concerns about the impact of additional deployments on its civilian infrastructure, including utilities, roads, and water supplies. Guam's location in the Western Pacific also requires construction of protection for U.S. forces and assets against typhoons. In the fall of 2006, PACOM officials briefed Guam on some aspects of an undisclosed draft plan for military expansion, the Integrated Military Development Plan, with possible military projects worth a total of about $15 billion.[18] In addition, Guam's size, remoteness, and conditions raised more questions about hosting and educating military dependents; training on Guam and with other units in Asia, Hawaii, or the west coast; and costs and time for extended logistical support and travel. Addressing another concern, a former commander of Marine Forces Pacific urged in 2007 that Guam's buildup include more than infrastructure to develop also human capital, communities, and the environment.[19]

Strategic Target. A concern is that Guam's higher military profile could increase its potential as a strategic target for terrorists and adversaries during a conflict. For example, potential PRC and DPRK missile attacks could raise Guam's need for missile defense and hardening of facilities. Some officials say that hardening could depend on the use of hangars, with less need of hardening for marines who deploy for training and more need of hardening for the air force's aircraft based at Andersen for power projection. A third option is selective hardening of some facilities.[20]

China is believed to have deployed missiles that could target forces on or near Guam, considered by China as part of the "Second Island Chain" from which it needs to break out of perceived U.S.-led "encirclement." China's missiles that could target Guam include the DF-3A (CSS-2) medium-range ballistic missiles (MRBMs) and land-attack cruise missiles (LACMs) launched from upgraded, longer-range H-6K bombers. China also has deployed DH-10 LACMs and DF-21D anti-ship ballistic missiles (ASBMs) to target aircraft carriers and other ships. While the DF-21D's initial range could be 1,500-2,000 km (930-1240 mi), a more advanced variant could extend the range to about 3,000 km and reach Guam. The PLA reportedly has the world's largest force of ground-launched LACMs, with about 100 LACMs entering the operational force each year and up to 500 LACMs by 2014. Moreover, the PRC reportedly has developed DF-26C intermediate-range ballistic missiles (IRBMs) with a range of about 4,000 km (2,500 mi) to be operational by 2015. In 2012, the PLA Navy started to conduct military activities, perhaps including surveillance, in the Exclusive Economic Zone (EEZ) around Guam.[21]

In addition, the DPRK has developed an IRBM with a range of more than 3,000 miles. There has been a question about whether North Korea deployed this IRBM. In 2008, South Korea's Defense White Paper stated that North Korea started to deploy its IRBM (Taepodong-X) with a range that

---

[18] *KUAM News*, September 12, 2006; *Pacific Daily News*, September 13, 2006; *Stars and Stripes*, September 17, 2006.

[19] W. C. "Chip" Gregson, "New Thinking Needed on Pacific Frontier," *Honolulu Advertiser*, December 7, 2007. From 2009 to 2011, Wallace "Chip" Gregson was the Assistant Secretary of Defense for Asian and Pacific Security Affairs.

[20] Author's consultations at PACOM in December 2013.

[21] Project 2049, "China's Evolving Conventional Strategic Strike Capability," September 14, 2009; Project 2049, "Evolving Aerospace Trends in the Asia-Pacific Region," May 25, 2010; *Global Times*, February 18, 2011; *Jane's Defense Weekly*, March 9, 2012; *Kanwa*, May 1, 2012; *Defense News*, January 31, 2013; *Nanfang Dushi Bao*, August 8, 2013; *Ta Kung Pao*, August 12, 2013; Project 2049, "China's Evolving Reconnaissance-Strike Capabilities," February 2014; *Free Beacon*, March 3, 2014; Office of the Secretary of Defense, "Annual Report to Congress: Military and Security Developments involving the PRC, 2014," June 2014.

could reach Guam. At a military parade in October 2010, North Korea showed a new IRBM (what some called Musudan), apparently deployed without flight testing in North Korea. The U.S. National Intelligence Council (NIC) reported to Congress in early 2011 that North Korea in 2010 continued to develop a mobile IRBM and did not report that it was deployed. Still, the Director of the Defense Intelligence Agency (DIA), Lieutenant General Ronald Burgess, Jr., testified to the Senate Armed Services Committee on March 10, 2011, that North Korea has tried to upgrade already deployed missiles that included IRBMs. In October 2012, the DPRK asserted that it has missiles that could strike South Korea, Japan, Guam, and the U.S. mainland.[22]

In February 2013, the DPRK announced a third nuclear test. The Defense Department, including Deputy Secretary Ashton Carter, announced that the Air Force flew B-52 strategic bombers from Andersen Air Force Base to South Korea on March 8 and 19 for "routine" exercises, extended deterrence, and a commitment to the alliance with South Korea. The DPRK's Korean People's Army then claimed that Guam's base for the B-52s was within range of its precision strike weapons and added a threat to "sweep away" Guam's Andersen base. On March 28, DPRK leader Kim Jong Un told the Strategic Rocket Force to prepare to hit military bases in Guam, Hawaii, and South Korea. Sources in Seoul reported that North Korea moved two Musudan IRBMs to its east coast that could be launched from mobile transporter erector launchers (TELs). The Defense Department announced on April 3 that it would deploy to Guam within weeks a Terminal High Altitude Area Defense (THAAD) ballistic missile defense system as a precautionary measure to improve defenses against the DPRK's missile threat. In early May, the DPRK reportedly removed the Musudan missiles away from the launch position. PACOM Commander Locklear said later in July that the missile's capability has not been demonstrated.[23]

Allies and Partners. Moreover, there was concern that Guam is still too distant from flash points in Asia and that the U.S. military could benefit from closer cooperation instead with allies and partners such as Singapore, Australia, the Philippines, and Japan.[24] Building up the U.S. presence in those countries could enhance alliances or partnerships, increase interoperability, and reduce costs for the United States. In 2010, Defense Secretary Gates wrote an article, calling for "building partner capacity" to help other countries to defend themselves, or if necessary, to fight alongside U.S. forces by providing them with equipment, training, and other security assistance. The stress would be on helping other countries provide for their own security.[25]

Later in 2010, Australia proposed that the U.S. military increase use of this ally's existing bases.[26] In April 2011, PACOM's Commander, Admiral Willard, testified to the House Armed Services Committee that the U.S. military has increased attention to Southeast and South Asia. He acknowledged that the U.S. force posture in Southeast Asia has involved mostly deployed U.S. forces, making it costly and inefficient. He sought to expand the U.S. presence in Southeast Asia beyond only Singapore. Willard also confirmed that Australia might further support the U.S.

---

[22] Sam Kim, "N. Korea Deploys Medium-Range Missiles, Bolsters Special Forces," *Yonhap*, Seoul, February 23, 2009; Joshua Pollack, "North Korea Debuts an IRBM," Arms Control Wonk blog, October 10, 2010; NIC, "Unclassified Report to Congress on the Acquisition of Technology Relating to Weapons of Mass Destruction and Advanced Conventional Munitions, Covering 1 January to 31 December 2010;" *KCNA*, Pyongyang, October 9, 2012; National Air and Space Intelligence Center (NASIC), "Ballistic and Cruise Missile Threat," July 2013.

[23] Ashton Carter, media availability in Seoul, South Korea, March 18; *Bloomberg*, March 19; *KCNA*, March 21, 27, and 28, 2013; *Yonhap*, April 4 and 11, 2013; *Reuters*, May 6, 2013; Defense Department, news briefing, July 11, 2013.

[24] Thomas Donnelly, "Rebasing, Revisited," American Enterprise Institute, December 2004.

[25] Robert Gates, "Helping Others Defend Themselves," *Foreign Affairs*, May/June 2010.

[26] Phil Stewart, "U.S. Military Moves in Asia Not Aimed At China: Gates," *Reuters*, November 7, 2010.

posture. In testimony the same month to the Senate Armed Services Committee, Willard stated that Marine Corps forces could rotate into northern Australia and other locations closer to Southeast Asia, in addition to marines in Japan, Guam, and Hawaii. Secretary Gates announced at a conference in June 2011 in Singapore that the United States will deploy Littoral Combat Ships there. On September 15, the United States and Australia held Ministerial Consultations (AUSMIN) at which the two sides, *inter alia*, agreed to strengthen potential defense cooperation that would entail greater U.S. access to Australian ranges, facilities, and ports; prepositioning of U.S. equipment in Australia; and combined activities in the Asian-Pacific region. Visiting Australia on November 16, President Obama announced that 2,500 marines will deploy on a rotational basis to Australia's Darwin base and the Air Force will rotate more aircraft to Australia. Thus, the changes would further disperse the U.S. forward presence, beyond moves to Guam.

One issue concerns whether more distributed forces in the Pacific would help or hurt deterrence. Another concern focuses on adequate space for the marines to train to maintain readiness. There also are logistical challenges in sustaining forces that are distributed daily over vast distances. Some in the Marine Corps have considered closer cooperation with the Philippines, including training. In June 2012, the Philippines reportedly welcomed resumed U.S. use of Subic Bay and Clark Air Base. However, the land has been privately developed in the two decades since Manila's opposition led to the U.S. withdrawal. Nonetheless, in June and July, Defense Secretary Panetta noted talks with the Philippines to explore other opportunities to enhance mutual capabilities, including sending U.S. forces on a rotational basis to strengthen maritime security. The Marine Corps Commandant, General James Amos, said in August that he discussed more frequent training exercises with commanders in the Philippines, Australia, Japan, and the ROK. Visiting Manila in April 2014, President Obama announced an Enhanced Defense Cooperation Agreement (EDCA). It would strengthen the U.S.-Philippine alliance, enhance the rotational presence of U.S. forces, facilitate humanitarian assistance and disaster relief, expand bilateral training, and support the Philippines' long-term military modernization for defense.[27]

Environmental Impact Statement (EIS) of 2010. In July 2010, the U.S. Navy's Joint Guam Program Office issued an Environmental Impact Statement (EIS) on implications of the buildup on Guam.[28] The detailed study estimated a higher population increase than a move of 8,000 marines to Guam. As noted above, the U.S.-Japan agreement of 2009 provided for 8,000 marines and 9,000 of their dependents to relocate from Okinawa to Guam. However, the EIS of 2010 estimated that a total of 8,552 marines plus 630 Army soldiers would form the 9,182 permanent military personnel to relocate to Guam. The total military population on Guam would increase by 30,190 (including 9,182 permanent military personnel, 9,950 dependents, 9,222 transient military personnel, and 1,836 civilian workers). In addition, construction workers and others could mean a total increase in population of about 79,000 at the peak in 2014, in this initial assumption. (After changes in the roadmap announced in April 2012, the Joint Guam Program Office announced on October 4 that it will prepare a new Supplemental Environmental Impact Statement. See below.)

---

[27] Travis Tritten, "Philippine Government Gives OK for US to Use Old Bases, Newspaper Reports," *Stars and Stripes*, June 7, 2012; Secretary of Defense, "Remarks at Shangri-la Dialogue," Singapore, June 2, 2012, and letter submitting to Congress an independent assessment on the U.S. defense posture in the Pacific, July 24, 2012; Richard Halloran, "Budget Axe to Hit U.S. Marine Corps," *Taipei Times*, August 16, 2012; Paul McLeary and Bethany Crudele, "U.S. Marines Battle 'Tyranny of Distance' in Pacific Pivot," *Defense News*, September 24, 2012; White House, "Fact Sheet: United States-Philippines Bilateral Relations," April 28, 2014.

[28] Joint Guam Program Office, "Final Environmental Impact Statement: Guam and CNMI Military Relocation," public release on July 29, 2010. This followed the Draft Environment Impact Statement issued in November 2009.

Training. The study completed in 2010 also found that Guam cannot accommodate all training for the relocated marines, and the nearby island of Tinian (100 miles away) could help to provide land for their training. There would be a challenge for sustaining operational readiness in training while limiting the time and expense to travel to train. The study found that "the training ranges currently planned for Guam and Tinian only replicate existing individual-skills training capabilities on Okinawa and do not provide for all requisite collective, combined arms, live and maneuver training the Marine Corps forces must meet to sustain core competencies. As with Marine Corps forces currently in Okinawa who must now travel to mainland Japan, other partner nations, and the U.S. to accomplish this requisite core competency training, the Marine Corps forces relocating from Okinawa to Guam would also have to use alternate locations to accomplish requisite core competency training." After a visit to Guam, Tinian, and Saipan in February 2010, Senator James Webb expressed concern about placing live-fire ranges on Guam for the Marine Corps and urged greater use of Tinian.[29] Also, Guam's Delegate Madeleine Bordallo expressed concern about a proposed firing range on Guam and urged the Pentagon to consider an alternative for a range on Tinian, at a hearing on March 15, 2011, of the House Armed Services Subcommittee on Readiness. The Assistant Secretary of the Navy for Energy, Installations, and Environment testified that certain training for the marines needs to be on the island of Guam.

In addition, the Navy would need a new deep-draft wharf at Apra Harbor to support a transient aircraft carrier. Third, the Army would relocate about 600 military personnel to establish and operate an Air and Missile Defense Task Force (AMDTF).

Record of Decision for EIS of 2010. However, as stated in the Record of Decision for the EIS that was issued in September 2010, the Navy and Army deferred decisions on a site for the marines' live-fire training range on Guam, a site for the transient aircraft carrier berth within Apra Harbor, and construction of an AMDTF on Guam. Also, the Record of Decision used an assumption that construction to support the marines' relocation would start in 2014 and not be completed until 2016. Moreover, the Record of Decision projected that instead of a peak of an increase of 79,178 people (including military personnel, dependents, and workers) in Guam in 2014, a "more realistic" projection would see a peak of 59,173 growth in population in 2015. The peak of 10,552 more marines on Guam would be reached in 2017 instead of 2014.[30]

Draft SEIS of 2014. Given the new force posture adjusted in 2012, the Department of the Navy issued a Draft Supplemental Environmental Impact Statement (SEIS) on April 18, 2014. The study planned for the relocation of about 5,000 marines with about 1,300 dependents to Guam over a longer period of 12 years (instead of 8,600 marines with 9,000 dependents relocating over five years assumed in the 2010 EIS). Two-thirds of the marines will be rotated to Guam, while their overall number will stay at about 5,000. Construction would involve moderate activity spread over 13 years (instead of an intense period of seven years). Guam would see fewer than 10,000 new residents at the peak of the construction boom (instead of more than 79,000). Projecting out to 2028, Guam would have about 7,400 additional residents (instead of more than 33,000). The Navy indicated its preferred alternative for the live-fire training range at Northwest Field on Andersen Air Force Base. The Final SEIS is expected in 2015, along with another

---

[29] Senator James Webb, "Proper Reengagement in Asia Requires a Strong Alliance with Japan, a Strong Relationship with the People of Guam," press release, February 19, 2010.

[30] "Record of Decision for Guam/Commonwealth of Northern Mariana Islands Military Relocation," September 2010.

Record of Decision and a master plan for the realignment. If approved by Congress, plans and approvals to start construction could take place in 2015.[31]

Costs. The original plan would not have involved only 10,552 marines. Congress expressed greater concern about expanding costs involved with moving more marines (estimated at 10,552) with additional army soldiers (estimated at 630) and civilian military workers (estimated at 1,836). That would have been an increase of 13,018 military and civilian personnel working for the Defense Department. Also, there could be expanded costs (for schools, health care, housing, transportation, etc.), if the option is used for personnel to be accompanied by dependents. The estimate of additional dependents increased from 9,000 under the U.S.-Japan agreement to 11,695 (9,000 Marine Corps dependents, 950 Army dependents, plus 1,745 civilian military dependents). Total personnel and dependent growth had been estimated at 24,713 from 2017 on, after completion of construction. At a hearing of the Senate Armed Services Committee on April 12, 2011, the chairman, Senator Carl Levin, expressed concern that the delays in the realignment could increase costs significantly. The Ranking Member, Senator John McCain, said that total investments by the United States and Japan for new bases for U.S. forces on both Okinawa and Guam could reach at least $30 billion. PACOM's Commander, Admiral Robert Willard, conceded that the delays and new requirements on Guam have raised uncertainty about the cost, which could be higher than $10.3 billion. Senator James Webb urged for greater clarity about the realignment and attention by the Senate. In his study in 1974 for Guam, Webb had called for a broader look at the total cost of the U.S. force structure in the Pacific that took into account any savings in consolidation of bases, more joint service uses, and the fact that bases in Guam are permanent bases on U.S. soil.[32] On May 26, 2011, Senators Levin, McCain, and Webb cited as support for their proposal to reexamine the plans for realignment a GAO report that estimated costs of over $27 billion to realign bases on Okinawa and Guam.[33] Then, as discussed above, the Joint Statement of April 2012 revised the U.S.-Japan cost of the marines' move to $8.6 billion.

In submitting to Congress the independent assessment by the Center for Strategic and International Studies (CSIS) on July 24, 2012, Defense Secretary Panetta acknowledged that there was still a need to work out details of the plan for future years but called for near-term investments in Guam to enable the early movement of some marines from Okinawa to Guam. The Secretary also urged investment in training ranges in Guam, the Commonwealth of the Northern Mariana Islands (CNMI), which includes Tinian, and potentially other unspecified areas.[34] Senators Levin, McCain, and Webb stated that Congress needs to be confident that the Defense Department's force planning and realignment are "realistic, workable, and affordable." In the House, Guam's Delegate Bordallo stressed that starting the investments in military and infrastructure projects would be critical to moving forward with the realignment on Guam, in part out of concern about the continued confidence of allies (specifically Japan) in U.S. planning.[35]

---

[31] Author's consultations at PACOM in December 2013; Department of the Navy, "Draft Supplemental Environmental Impact Statement," April 18, 2014; *Stars and Stripes*, April 18, 2014; *Guam News*, April 18, 2014.

[32] James Webb, "The Future Land Needs of the U.S. Military on Guam," Guam Bureau of Planning, July 24, 1974.

[33] Senator Carl Levin, "GAO Report Validates Recommendations for Bases in East Asia; Action Needed to Re-examine DoD Planning"; Senator Jim Webb, "GAO Findings a Call to Action on Realignment of Military Bases in East Asia," May 26, 2011.

[34] Secretary of Defense, letter to submit the independent assessment pursuant to the FY2012 NDAA, July 24, 2012. The non-governmental, independent assessment did not represent the official position of the Defense Department.

[35] Senator Jim Webb, "Statement of Senators Levin, McCain, and Webb on CSIS Asia Report," July 27, 2012; Delegate Madeleine Bordallo, "House Armed Services Readiness Subcommittee Addresses CSIS Report on U.S. Force Posture in the U.S. Pacific Command Area of Responsibility," August 1, 2012.

Naval and Air Assets. As another concern, the marines on Guam would need naval assets for transportation for both deployments and exercises. Options include basing in Guam another Amphibious Ready Group (ARG) with amphibious ships of the Navy to transport a Marine Expeditionary Unit (MEU). Another consideration would homeport in Guam the new non-combatant sealift Joint High Speed Vessel (JHSV). Since 2001, the III MEF in Okinawa already has experience with using a leased theater support ship called "Westpac Express." The marines used this fast, roll-on/roll-off ship to deploy with helicopters to reinforce Guam's defense after the 9/11 terrorist attacks in 2001.[36] Sealift or airlift could come from Hawaii or California.[37]

In submitting to Congress the independent assessment by CSIS in July 2012, Defense Secretary Panetta acknowledged that additional lift will be required to support the dispersed MAGTFs throughout the Pacific region and that the realignment of the Marine Corps units will be more distributed than that in the status quo and previous plans. The Secretary disagreed with the independent assessment that the marines could rotate fewer than about 5,000 marines to Guam, insisting that the MAGTF would be one of four (in Guam, Okinawa, Australia, and Hawaii) that would be expected to respond rapidly to low-end and high-end contingencies by combining command, maritime, ground, air, logistics, and lift capabilities that can deploy together.

The independent assessment recommended, *inter alia*, addition of one or more SSNs at Guam, deployment of an additional ARG in the Pacific region, increase in roll-on/roll-off ships and aerial tankers in the Pacific, deployment of missile defense assets (THAAD and PAC-3) to Guam, runway repair capability at Guam, dispersal of tanker aircraft rather than hardening, and additional assets for the Contingency Response Group and fuel pipelines at Andersen Air Force Base. At a hearing of the House Armed Services Subcommittee on Readiness on August 1, 2012, Defense Department officials acknowledged that the department could consider enhancing the posture with Guam as a strategic hub but cautioned that it must consider global requirements. Conferees on the FY2013 NDAA (P.L. 112-239) expressed congressional concerns about the need for a clear plan for airlift and sealift to meet Guam's operational and logistical challenges.

Outside Workers. Some have noted a concern about the potential introduction of temporary outside workers to Guam during construction for the defense buildup. In 2009, Representative Neil Abercrombie of Hawaii urged a preference for American workers.[38] Regarding defense policy, some have raised security considerations of the country of origin of any foreign workers, including China. For example, in 2009, Guam's Governor Felix Camacho said that it was likely that foreign workers could come from skilled labor in the Philippines, if local labor is insufficient. He said that China's workers would not be hired "because of security concerns related to work on military bases."[39] Workers outside of Guam could be hired from Hawaii, the U.S. mainland, American Samoa, Northern Mariana Islands, Freely Associated States, or other places.

Military Readiness. At a hearing of the House Armed Services Subcommittee on Readiness on March 15, 2011, Representative Randy Forbes and Guam's Delegate Bordallo focused on the issue of whether U.S. forces in the Pacific have sufficient military readiness, including in the realignment on Guam. Assistant Secretary of the Navy for Energy, Installations, and Environment Jackalyne Pfannenstiel testified that the first focus would be on assuring adequate land to be able

---

[36] Consultations with PACOM in Honolulu in November 2010 and Pentagon in Washington in December 2010.

[37] Remarks by retired Lieutenant General, USMC, George Trautman III, at Heritage Foundation, May 3, 2012.

[38] Neil Abercrombie, "Why Construction on Guam is Right for Americans," letter to *Washington Post*, July 13, 2009.

[39] "Guam Governor Expects Filipinos to Fill Jobs," *The Star*, July 1, 2009.

to train the marines as they arrive in Guam. Major General (USMC) Randolph Alles, PACOM's Director of Strategic Planning and Policy (J-5), acknowledged concern about the vulnerability of above-ground stored fuel on Guam. Later, on January 28, 2014, at a hearing on the strategic "rebalance" to Asia at the House Armed Services Committee, Delegate Bordallo asked about readiness, and the Joint Staff's Director for Strategic Plans and Policy, Vice Admiral Frank Pandolfe, expressed concerns about the consequences of budget cuts on force readiness.

Review of Force Structure. There could be attention to how Guam fits in more broadly to the U.S. force structure in the Pacific. Senator James Webb called for more attention to "all the players out there in the region" regarding the realignment, at a hearing on April 12, 2011, of the Senate Armed Services Committee.[40] As Senator Levin said at the Senate Armed Services Committee's hearing in April, "the details of the plans for Okinawa are many and complex, as are the details of the associated military buildup on Guam. That said, because these actions will affect the U.S. military's strategic positioning well into the future, it is important that these issues be discussed and resolved." Senator Webb said, "I have a concern that we are at this point allowing the process to be determined in many ways simply by the momentum of defense planners at a time when a lot of these pieces are in question. So I hope we can have a hearing. I'm going to be traveling to Korea and then into Guam again and Okinawa in the coming weeks, and Chairman Levin is going to accompany me to Guam and Okinawa. I think it will be a very important set of visits and perhaps we can try to find ways to at least clarify this matter and move forward."

Subsequently, trying to move forward, Senators Levin, McCain, and Webb called in May 2011 for a re-examination of plans to restructure military forces in South Korea, Japan, and Guam. They critiqued the planned realignment as "unrealistic, unworkable, and unaffordable." As another objective, the Senators sought to reassure "Japan, Korea, and other countries that the United States strongly supports a continuous and vigorous U.S. presence in the region" as well as "strong bilateral alliances."[41] They also noted consideration of Japan's enormous financial burden that resulted from the earthquake, tsunami, and nuclear disaster in March 2011. Contrary to much press reporting that stressed the proposal as criticizing plans and trying to "freeze" or to "put on hold" the plans, a goal of the Senators' proposal to review basing plans was to address concerns, cut costs, and make progress at a time when the realignment to Guam faced an impasse and a strong U.S. military presence remained critical in the Asian-Pacific region. For Guam, the Senators proposed to base a permanently assigned headquarters (with family accompaniment) for a "stripped-down" presence of the Marine Corps, but bolstered by deployments of rotating combat troops that would be home-based elsewhere. They noted that rotating units into and out of Guam from a home base such as in Hawaii or California (and thus leaving families at those bases) "would make a strong difference in terms of infrastructure costs for schools, medical, recreational facilities, and housing." The Senators also recommended that the Defense Department examine the feasibility of moving Marine Corps assets at Futenma into Kadena Air Base while dispersing some Air Force assets now at Kadena to other areas in the Pacific region, including Andersen Air Force Base in Guam. They further noted that Kadena's 6,000-acre ammunition storage site could be downsized by making use of two ammunition storage areas already located in Guam.

---

[40] Webb started in the 1970s to look strategically at Guam's place in the U.S. defense posture in the Pacific, writing in 1974 that "it is quite conceivable that in ten to twenty years the entire U.S. Pacific presence will be centered on a Guam-Tinian axis." He had proposed a shift of the Marine Corps from Okinawa to Tinian. He lamented that "Guam has been a loyal, though often unrecognized and ignored, segment of the American system." James Webb, Jr., *Micronesia and U.S. Pacific Strategy: A Blueprint for the 1980s,* Praeger Publishers, 1974.

[41] Senate Armed Services Committee, "Senators Levin, McCain, Webb Call for Re-examination of Military Basing Plans in East Asia," May 11, 2011.

Guam's Delegate Madeleine Bordallo promptly issued a press release on the same day. She focused on the Senators' "re-examination" of the plans for bases in Guam and elsewhere. She also focused on the Senators' appraisal of Guam's "strategic importance." She saw their recommendation as another opportunity for the Defense Department to further clarify plans and rationale concerning the bases. However, she seemed to raise concerns that consolidating Marine Corps assets from Futenma to Kadena Air Base needs to be addressed directly between the U.S. Government and Japan's Government, because it would require "serious changes" to the Defense Posture Review Initiative (DPRI). She also raised concern that moving air assets from Kadena Air Base to Andersen Air Force Base would require "careful attention to the balance among forces on Guam so that additional air assets and associated personnel do not overload and unduly strain [Guam's] infrastructure." Further, she raised concern that a "transient presence" of marines on Guam would reduce family housing but also reduce funds that would come from permanently stationed forces. In addition, she expressed concern about reducing military families and their ties to Guam. At the same time, Delegate Bordallo cited a mention in the proposal about an issue related to firing ranges and reiterated her call for the Defense Department to certify a national security requirement for such ranges. She also highlighted the Senators' reference to Guam's "clear message" about its need for federal funds to build up its infrastructure outside of the bases. According to her, when the time came for the conference on the National Defense Authorization Act, the Senators "will now better see" the need for her proposal to give the Defense Department the authority to transfer funds to support local infrastructure. Finally, she assured her constituents that the Senators did not propose to stop Guam's buildup and that she took their view to be in line with views in the House, namely, that the buildup should be "done right."[42]

In the House Armed Services Committee, Representative Randy Forbes and Delegate Bordallo wrote to Secretary Panetta on September 30, 2011, to express concerns about the realignment of forces, particularly to Guam. They sought a master plan for and senior-level attention to the realignment as a top priority. Under Secretary of Defense for Policy Michele Flournoy finally replied on December 13, acknowledging that the Pentagon was re-examining options for Guam. Finally, in the Joint Statement of February 8, 2012, the Obama Administration reached an agreement with Japan to "adjust" the Realignment Roadmap, as discussed above.

Local Concerns. Related, there has been an issue of whether policy makers have addressed Guam's concerns about the scope and pace of the construction, as expressed by the local people or their elected officials. For example, at a hearing of the House Armed Services Committee on February 3, 2010, Guam's Delegate Madeleine Bordallo urged Secretary Gates to take into account the concerns of the local community that the buildup would be "done right," including in the impact on the environment. Senator Webb visited Tokyo, Okinawa, and Guam in February 2010, in part to listen to various people about the U.S. realignment in the region. He also urged a more open discussion about the realistic timeline for the realignment and buildup on Guam by 2014. He urged sensitivity to the stress of the people and limitations of space on Guam, including over the issue of whether the military should have more land beyond the current one-third of the island.[43] On April 25-26, 2011, Senators James Webb and Carl Levin visited Guam and met with

---

[42] Madeleine Bordallo, "Reaction to Senators' Call for Re-examination of Military Basing Plans in East Asia," May 11, 2011.

[43] Senator James Webb, "Proper Reengagement in Asia Requires a Strong Alliance with Japan, a Strong Relationship with the People of Guam," press release, February 19, 2010.

local officials, who assured them that Guam's people support the defense buildup but with local gains and improved communication of information from the Defense Department.[44]

Allies and Partners

The U.S.-Japan Security Consultative Committee envisioned in 2005 that Guam would provide expanded opportunities for training for Japan's SDF and improved interoperability. For combined training and engagement with allies and partners, Guam has provided valuable and less constrained airspace and bombing ranges for the air forces of Japan, Thailand, Singapore, South Korea, and Australia. In October 2011, exercises with fighters based at Marine Corps Air Station Iwakuni (on Japan's mainland) moved for the first time to Guam from Kadena Air Base in Okinawa. In February 2012, Andersen Air Force Base hosted an air exercise (Cope North 2012) among U.S., Japanese, and Australian Air Forces, with Australia's participation for the first time. In August-September 2012, Japan's Ground Self-Defense Force joined U.S. marines in exercises in Guam and Tinian. For the first time, South Korea's Air Force observed the Cope North exercise (its humanitarian assistance and disaster relief portion) in February 2013.

Also, Taiwan reportedly has asked to fly to Guam for training. Taiwan's F-16 fighter pilots already train at Luke Air Force Base in Arizona. Taiwan has other options for both training and operations (such as humanitarian missions) to fly to nations in the western Pacific that keep diplomatic ties with Taipei. Taiwan could help to improve and extend their runways if needed.

South Korea. The Guam Integrated Military Development Plan, parts of which were reported in October 2006, indicated that U.S. Army units withdrawn from South Korea were not likely to be stationed on Guam. The Pentagon's restructuring plan reportedly intended to maintain U.S. air power in South Korea, particularly the three squadrons of F-16 fighters based at Osan Air Base.[45]

In September 2008, Secretary of the Navy Donald Winter submitted a report that envisioned a consolidation of the expeditionary training centers of the U.S. Pacific Air Forces (PACAF) from South Korea to Guam.[46] However, the Record of Decision for Guam of 2010 did not mention South Korea. In testimony to the House Armed Services Committee on April 6, 2011, PACOM's Commander, Admiral Willard, testified that PACAF has planned to use Guam as the "hub" for air force assets in strike and refueling missions in the Asian-Pacific region. Also, PACAF has been building some projects to set up the Pacific Regional Training Center at Guam.

There could be an option for South Korea to contribute to the cost of the defense buildup on Guam. Some officials have tied the buildup to North Korea's threat. Deputy Assistant Secretary of Defense for East Asia Michael Schiffer testified to Congress in March 2010 that the implementation of the 2006 Realignment Roadmap would help meet shared security challenges, including the threat posed by North Korea. Just after North Korea launched artillery attacks on South Korea's Yeonpyeong Island in November 2010, Guam's Delegate Madeleine Bordallo issued a statement that she received a briefing on the situation in South Korea from the Defense

---

[44] "U.S. Senators Webb, Levin Hear Guam Concerns," *Guam Pacific Daily News*, April 27, 2011; "Senator Jim Webb's East Asia Trip: Record of Activities and Achievements, April 16-29, 2011," press release, April 29, 2011.

[45] Murayama Kohei, "U.S. to Triple Troops in Guam, but No Earlier Than 2010 for Marines," *Kyodo*, October 3, 2006; Bill Gertz, "More Muscle, With Eye on China," *Washington Times*, April 20, 2006; Robert Burns, "U.S. Air Power in East Asia Has Grown," *Associated Press*, October 11, 2006.

[46] Donald Winter, "Report on Department of Defense Planning Efforts for Guam," September 15, 2008.

Department. She also asserted that "this attack by North Korea is a reminder of the importance of the United States remaining a vigilant and visible power in the Asia-Pacific region. Further it highlights the importance of realigning our military forces in this region to be better postured to address destabilizing events." Senator Jim Webb delivered a speech in Tokyo in February 2011 in which he noted that, given regional tension in the Koreas and elsewhere in Asia, "it is extremely important for Japan and the United States to work to maintain a strategic stability in this region and also for us to take advantage of the willingness of South Korea to join in this effort."[47]

Japan. Under the U.S.-Japan Security Treaty, U.S. concerns involved possible conflict between China and Japan over their competing claims to the Senkaku islands (called Diaoyu islands by China) in the East China Sea. Taiwan, asserting itself as the Republic of China, also claims the islands as the Diaoyutai islands. The United States administered the islands after World War II and turned them over to Japanese administration in 1972. Officials of the Bill Clinton, George W. Bush, and Barack Obama Administrations have stated that the Senkaku Islands fall under the scope of the U.S.-Japan alliance. Japan's concern increased in September 2005, when the PLA Navy deployed five ships to the disputed area in the East China Sea with competing territorial and oil claims. After China escalated tension with Japan in wake of a PRC fishing boat's collision with Japan's patrol boats in September 2010, Secretary of State Hillary Clinton and Defense Secretary Gates explicitly assured Japan of the U.S. position that the Senkaku Islands are covered by the defense treaty. During China-Japan tension over the islands in September 2012, Defense Secretary Leon Panetta visited Tokyo (before Beijing), where he said that the United States stands by the treaty obligations, which are longstanding and unchanged. Visiting Tokyo on April 6, 2014, Defense Secretary Chuck Hagel said that "I restated the principles that govern longstanding U.S. policy, U.S. policy on the Senkaku Islands and other islands. And we affirmed that since they are under Japan's administrative control, they fall under Article 5 of our mutual security treaty." Visiting Japan later in April, President Obama stated that the U.S. "treaty commitment to Japan's security is absolute, and Article 5 [of the U.S.-Japan Treaty of Mutual Cooperation and Security] covers all territories under Japan's administration, including the Senkaku Islands."[48]

After China's military announced an "East China Sea Air Defense Identification Zone (ADIZ)" that covered the Senkaku Islands on November 23, 2013, the U.S. Air Force flew two B-52 bombers from Guam through that "ADIZ" in defiance of China's rules for notification. The bombers were unarmed. A Pentagon spokesman said that "we have conducted operations in the area of the Senkakus. We have continued to follow our normal procedures, which include not

---

[47] Michael Schiffer's testimony before the House Foreign Affairs Subcommittee on Asia, the Pacific, and the Global Environment, March 17, 2010; Guam Delegate Madeleine Bordallo's press release, November 23, 2010; Senator Jim Webb, keynote address, New Shimoda Conference, Tokyo, Japan, February 22, 2011.

[48] CRS Report R42761, *Senkaku (Diaoyu/Diaoyutai) Islands Dispute: U.S. Treaty Obligations*, by Mark E. Manyin; "U.S.-Japan Treaty Covers Disputed Isles," *Reuters*, November 28, 1996; Yoichi Funabashi, "Maintain the Armitage Doctrine Quietly," *Asahi Shimbun*, February 2, 2004; State Department's spokesperson, press briefing, March 24, 2004; "Clinton Tells Maehara Senkakus Subject to Japan-U.S. Security Pact," *Kyodo*, September 23, 2010; Defense Department, "News Briefing with Secretary Gates and Admiral Mullen," September 23, 2010; White House, "press briefing," New York, September 23, 2010; State Department, "Joint Press Availability with Japanese Foreign Minister Seiji Maehara," Honolulu, October 27, 2010; Defense Department, "Joint Press Conference with Secretary Panetta and Japanese Minister of Defense Morimoto," Tokyo, September 17, 2012; Defense Department, "Joint Press Conference with Secretary of Defense Chuck Hagel and Japanese Minister of Defense Itsunori Onodera," Tokyo, April 06, 2014; Defense Department, "Remarks by Secretary Hagel in a Question-and-Answer Session at the People's Liberation Army National Defense University," Beijing, China, April 8, 2014; President Obama, Interview published in *Yomiuri Shimbun's Japan News*, April 23, 2014; White House, "Joint Press Conference with President Obama and Prime Minister Abe of Japan," Tokyo, Japan, April 24, 2014; White House, "U.S.-Japan Joint Statement," April 25, 2014.

---

filing flight plans, not radioing ahead, and not registering our frequencies."[49] Nonetheless, while conveying continuity of operations, sustained support for Japan, and defiance of the PRC's "ADIZ," the bombers flew on a long-planned training flight. Secretary of Defense Hagel stated on November 23 that the ADIZ is a destabilizing attempt to alter the status quo and will not change how the U.S. military conducts operations. Hagel reiterated that the U.S.-Japan Mutual Defense Treaty applies to the Senkaku Islands. Speaking by phone with Japan's Defense Minister Itsunori Onodera on November 27, Secretary Hagel stressed the top priority of resolving remaining issues in the realignment of forces.

China

Building Guam as a strategic hub has played a critical role in balancing U.S. security interests in responding to and cooperating with China as well as in shaping China's perceptions and conduct. The Obama Administration's strategy has sought to shape China's rise as a power that is peaceful, responsible, and respectful of international rules and laws. However, China's Sino-centric civilian and military commentators have suspected the defense buildup on Guam as aimed at China. Some skeptics of U.S. policy ask whether there is a coherent strategy for countering China's challenges, while other critics worry that U.S. actions and statements would raise tensions with China.

Washington and Beijing have long differed over China's threats to use the People's Liberation Army (PLA) against Taiwan. U.S. policy on helping Taiwan's self-defense is governed not by a defense treaty but by the Taiwan Relations Act (TRA), P.L. 96-8. Moreover, some concerns about the PLA's accelerated modernization since the Taiwan Strait Crisis of 1995-1996 have expanded beyond Taiwan to include PLA preparations for possible conflicts with the United States, Japan, and others. In Southeast Asia, China claims much of the South China Sea as well as the disputed Spratly and Paracel Islands in that sea as its "sovereign territory." The PLA has raised attention to Guam and has been building up its submarine force (both nuclear-powered and diesel-electric). In November 2004, the PLA Navy sent a Han-class nuclear attack submarine to waters off Guam before intruding into Japan's territorial water.[50] Further, the PLA's rising power has implications beyond Asia. The National Military Strategy of 2011 stated concerns about China's assertiveness in space, cyberspace, the Yellow Sea, East China Sea, and South China Sea. By early 2012, the Director of National Intelligence (DNI) testified to Congress that "Many of Beijing's military capability goals have now been realized, resulting in impressive military might. Other goals remain longer term, but the PLA is receiving the funding and political support to transform the PLA into a fully modern force, capable of sustained operations in Asia and beyond."[51]

In 2007, PACOM Commander Admiral Timothy Keating visited Guam and acknowledged that its defense buildup was partly due to concerns about tension over Taiwan and North Korea. At the same time, he stressed U.S. transparency, saying the buildup was not "under the cover of darkness." In answer to Senator Webb about the PLA's expanding activities at a hearing in March 2008, Keating testified that during his first visit to China (in May 2007), the PLA Navy proposed—in seriousness or in jest—that as it acquires aircraft carriers, it would take the Pacific west of Hawaii while the U.S. Navy would cover east of Hawaii.[52] Deputy Assistant Secretary of

---

[49] "Defying China, U.S. Bombers and Japanese Planes Fly Through New Air Zone," *Reuters*, November 27, 2013.

[50] *Kyodo World Service*, November 16, 2004.

[51] James Clapper, testimony on worldwide threats to the Senate Select Committee on Intelligence, January 31, 2012.

[52] Audrey McAvoy, "U.S. Pacific Commander Says Taiwan is Factor in Guam Buildup," *AP*, April 15, 2007; Senate Armed Services Committee, hearing on the FY2009 Budget for PACOM and USFK, March 11, 2008.

Defense for East Asia Michael Schiffer testified to Congress in March 2010 that the implementation of the 2006 Realignment Roadmap would help meet shared security challenges, including the threat posed by North Korea as well as uncertainty posed by the PLA's "rapid" modernization. In the same month in answer to Senator Daniel Akaka, PACOM's Commander, Admiral Willard, cited the PLA Air Force's fighters and air defense systems for U.S. deployment of F-22 fighters in the Pacific, including at Guam's Andersen Air Force Base.[53] The Commander of Pacific Air Forces, General Gary North, acknowledged in October 2011 that U.S. forces needed to watch China's "expansive claims" in the South China Sea. He added that the three Global Hawk reconnaissance drones based at Guam can stay airborne for over 30 hours.[54]

However, the impasse with Japan that started in 2009 over the realignment to Guam raised increased concerns about PRC misperceptions of weakened U.S. alliances that could affect stability. Also, with the planned move of significant numbers of marines from Japan to Guam, the PRC could misperceive pushing a U.S. retreat from the "first island chain" to the "second island chain." In Congress, Senator James Webb said in a speech in Tokyo in February 2011 that Northeast Asia is the only place in the world where the interests of the United States, Russia, China, and Japan intersect. He noted that the U.S.-Japan relationship resulted in regional stability. Concerning China, Senator Webb said that when the Soviet Union collapsed, the United States became "overexposed and unprepared" for the way that China has expanded. While affecting the U.S. economy, China's rise also has incrementally affected regional stability. He urged careful handling of the realignment of bases to avoid giving the wrong signals for strategic stability.[55] Also, a retired rear admiral wrote in May 2012 that the delinking of the marines' move to Guam from the dispute over Futenma was a "welcome development," because officials could focus the attention of the U.S.-Japan alliance on its most significant challenge, namely, the change in the strategic balance in Asia due to PLA efforts to extend its defense perimeter farther out to sea. In this competition, the PRC tries to deny access, while the United States and others assure access.[56]

QDRs and Air-Sea Battle Concept. Under President Obama, the Pentagon issued a QDR in February 2010 that announced the development of a new Air-Sea Battle Concept, as noted above. The QDR's discussion of that concept did not name China. Nevertheless, some analysts discussed the Air-Sea Battle Concept as a way to counter the PLA's rising capabilities in anti-access and area-denial (A2/AD) (to slow or keep farther away U.S. forces in moving to a theater of operations and to impede U.S. freedom of action in maneuvering within a theater). A year later in February 2011, PACOM's Commander, Admiral Robert Willard, said that the Defense Department added the Marine Corps into the study of the new doctrine. In March, Secretary Gates acknowledged that China, North Korea, and Iran are countries that pose emerging asymmetric threats by developing capabilities that appear designed to neutralize the advantages of the U.S. military in unfettered freedom of movement and projection of power to any region. Gates added that, with the new concept, the Air Force and Navy would leverage each other's capabilities to overcome future A2/AD threats.[57] At a hearing of the House Armed Services

---

[53] Testimonies before the House Foreign Affairs Subcommittee on Asia, the Pacific, and the Global Environment, March 17, 2010; and Senate Armed Services Committee, March 26, 2010.

[54] David Fulghum, "Recon Needs Grow for South China Sea Region," *Aviation Week*, October 21, 2011.

[55] Senator James Webb, "Revitalizing Japan-U.S. Strategic Partnership for a Changing World," keynote address, New Shimoda Conference, Tokyo, Japan, February 22, 2011.

[56] Michael McDevitt, "The Evolving Maritime Security Environment in East Asia: Implications for the U.S.-Japan Alliance," PacNet #33, Pacific Forum, May 31, 2012.

[57] Michael McDevitt, "The 2010 QDR and Asia: Messages for the Region," *Asia Pacific Bulletin*, East-West Center, March 11, 2010; Center for Strategic and Budgetary Assessments, "AirSea Battle: A Point-of-Departure Operational (continued...)

Subcommittee on Readiness on March 15, 2011, Major General (USMC) Randolph Alles, PACOM's Director of Strategic Planning and Policy (J-5), explicitly testified that the new concept addresses A2/AD but is broader than a focus on China. The concept would address security situations around the world. On November 9, 2011, the Defense Department announced the establishment of an office on the Air-Sea Battle Concept, in order to integrate air and naval combat capabilities of the Navy, Air Force, and Marine Corps to counter A2/AD challenges. In May 2013, the Air-Sea Battle Office issued an unclassified summary of the Air-Sea Battle Concept, stressing that it is not a strategy. The Army, Marine Corps, Navy, and Air Force collaborated on a concept to develop networked, integrated forces capable of attack-in-depth to disrupt, destroy, and defeat adversary forces. With potential implications for Guam, the concept assumed that adversaries will attack U.S. military equipment, networks, and people as well as bases from which U.S. and allied forces operate.

The QDR of 2014 assessed that "in the coming years, countries such as China will continue seeking to counter U.S. strengths using [A2/AD] approaches and by employing other new cyber and space control technologies. Additionally, these and other states continue to develop sophisticated integrated air defenses that can restrict access and freedom of maneuver in waters and airspace beyond territorial limits." The QDR reaffirmed the marines' move to Guam.[58]

"Rebalancing" Strategy. At the start of 2012, President Obama and Defense Secretary Panetta issued the new Defense Strategic Guidance on how to maintain U.S. military superiority in the face of budget cuts and to "rebalance" priorities, posture, and presence to stress more attention to Asia as well as the Middle East. The strategy explicitly cited concerns about China's rising military power as potentially causing "friction" in Asia and about U.S. power projection against A2/AD challenges, particularly from China and Iran.[59] However, the strategy did not mention the Air-Sea Battle Concept. Then, the Chairman of the Joint Chiefs of Staff issued on January 17 a new Joint Operational Access Concept (JOAC). Thus, the initiative expanded from a focus on the Navy and Air Force, to add the Marine Corps, and to cover all services. At the Shangri-la Dialogue of defense ministers in June 2012, Defense Secretary Panetta provided some details for the new strategy, saying that, by 2020, 60% of the Navy's vessels would be assigned to the Pacific, including 6 of 11 aircraft carriers. However, some specialists are concerned that there might be limits in the total numbers of available assets given budget constraints and that the goal is not new. As noted above, the QDR of 2006 called for a greater presence in the Pacific. Still, President Obama said that the "pivot" to Asia stresses the United States as a Pacific power.[60] During a visit to Guam in July 2012, Deputy Secretary of Defense Carter cited the "strategic hub" of Guam in the current context of the rebalancing strategy, though Guam's buildup started years

---

(...continued)

Concept," May 18, 2010; Bruce Rolfsen, "Air Force-Navy Team May Counter China Threat," *Navy Times*, May 23, 2010; Bill Gertz, "Military to Bolster Its Forces in the Pacific," *Washington Times*, February 18, 2011; Robert Gates, speech at the Air Force Academy, Colorado Springs, March 4, 2011; "Team Links AirSea Battle to China," *Inside the Pentagon*, June 9, 2011; Dave Majumdar, "U.S. Air Force's Bomber Will be One Aircraft, Not Many," *Defense News*, July 18, 2011; Tony Capaccio, "Panetta Reviewing Air-Sea Battle Plan Summary, Greenert Says," *Bloomberg*, July 26, 2011. On one of the first studies of China's A2/AD strategy, see *Enter the Dragon's Lair* (Rand Corporation, 2007). For skeptical views: Thomas Barnett, "Big-War Thinking in a Small-War Era," *China Security*, November 2010; J. Noel Williams, "Air-Sea Battle: An Operational Concept Looking for a Strategy," *AFJ*, September 2011; Dave Majumdar, "U.S. AirSea Battle Takes Shape Amid Debate," *Defense News*, October 10, 2011.

[58] Defense Department, "Quadrennial Defense Review," February 2010; "Quadrennial Defense Review," March 2014.

[59] Defense Department, "Sustaining U.S. Global Leadership: Priorities for 21st Century Defense," January 5, 2012.

[60] White House, "Remarks by President Obama and President Aquino of the Philippines," June 8, 2012.

before. Carter later explained that the strategy is "not about China" but a peaceful Pacific region and involves shifting capacity and investment to the Pacific, including to Guam.[61]

In his remarks, Panetta said that the rebalancing strategy also envisions investments in special operation forces (SOF). The Special Operations Command Pacific (SOCPAC) commands the Naval Special Warfare Unit 1 (SEALS) on Guam. SOCPAC supports the strategic rebalancing, by expanding engagements and SOF rotational presence. In the first half of 2014, a Marines Special Operations Company is rotating to Guam for the first time to work with the Navy SEALS.[62]

"Rebalance" and Engagement with China. Still, a policy challenge has been to avoid conflict with China and deter aggression by China and to assure that a U.S. goal is to cooperate in any converging interests with this rising power as a peaceful, responsible, and rules-based country. Indeed, China has benefitted from U.S. preservation of peace and prosperity in the region. The PRC leadership acknowledged to President Obama in November 2009, in the first U.S.-PRC Joint Statement in 12 years, that "China welcomes the United States as an Asia-Pacific nation that contributes to peace, stability, and prosperity in the region." The Administration has sought to build "strategic trust" and a "positive, cooperative, and comprehensive" relationship with Beijing.

In Guam's buildup, the Commander of Pacific Air Forces said in 2005 that the PLA's modernization gave him "pause for interest" but did not make a difference in significant force redeployment.[63] Also, in 2006, Guam became a focal point for improving the military-to-military relationship with China. To blunt charges that Guam's buildup targeted China, PACOM's Commander, Admiral Fallon, invited PLA observers to the U.S. "Valiant Shield" exercise that brought three aircraft carriers to waters off Guam in June 2006. The PLA Navy sent a Deputy Chief of Staff and specialist in submarine operations to lead the observers, who also boarded an aircraft carrier and visited Guam's air and naval bases. In May 2008, two C-17 transport aircraft flew supplies from Guam to China for earthquake relief. Also in 2008, the Deputy PACOM Commander addressed the question of whether China posed a threat and if China could see Guam as a threat, and he said that while the United States had concerns about China's military buildup, "that's not why we're basing forces in Guam." He noted that the forces were already based and standing ready in the Pacific, with new adjustments in U.S. posture.[64] While in Australia in late 2010, Defense Secretary Gates stated that moves to strengthen the U.S. military presence in the region were more about relationships with the rest of Asia than about China.[65]

The Obama Administration has attempted to clarify some aspects of the strategy. The Chief of Naval Operations (CNO), Admiral Jonathan Greenert, clarified in early 2012 that the new strategy to rebalance with a greater focus on the Asian-Pacific region would not mean a large increase in the naval presence in the Western Pacific. Greenert said, "it's not a big naval buildup in the Far East. We're there. We have been there. We will be there." He said that the U.S. Navy will engage closer with the PLA and cooperate more with allies and partners to promote a rules-based order and maintain freedom of navigation. In answer to Senator Daniel Akaka at a hearing in February, the Chairman of the Joint Chiefs of Staff, General Martin Dempsey, testified that the rebalancing (not a pivot) in the strategy actually offers the opportunity to expand engagement

---

[61] Ashton Carter, "The U.S. Strategic Rebalance to Asia: a Defense Perspective," New York City, August 1, 2012.

[62] Consultation with SOCPAC, August 2012 and January 2014.

[63] Interview with General Paul Hester, *Inside the Air Force*, May 6, 2005.

[64] Interview with Lieutenant General Dan Leaf (USAF), *Asia-Pacific Defense Forum*, 1st Quarter 2008.

[65] Phil Stewart, "U.S. Military Moves in Asia Not Aimed At China: Gates," *Reuters*, November 7, 2010.

with the PLA. At another hearing, Defense Secretary Leon Panetta answered Representative Hank Johnson about the risk of an increasingly adversarial military competition by testifying that the U.S. military needs to engage with the PLA from a position of strength and with preservation of the presence in the Pacific. In June, at the meeting of defense ministers in Singapore, Secretary Panetta stressed that defense policy is only part of the "rebalancing" of the entire U.S. Government. General Dempsey said that repositioning forces is not the essence of the rebalancing strategy, but rather more attention, more engagement, and more quality. In submitting an independent assessment on the U.S. posture in the Pacific on July 24, Secretary Panetta wrote to Congress that the strategy calls for comprehensively "rebalancing defense, diplomatic, and economic resources toward the Asia-Pacific region." In March 2013, National Security Advisor Tom Donilon spoke about the rebalancing with a goal to build a constructive relationship with China (including through military-to-military contacts). He said that the Administration disagreed with the premise that a rising power and an established power are destined for conflict.[66]

In short, one issue has concerned whether the Administration's "rebalancing" credibly conveyed a comprehensive strategy in a Whole of Government approach.[67] A related issue has asked whether the message effectively conveyed cooperating with or countering China. A third issue has asked whether the United States realistically sustains the rhetorical intentions, given budget constraints.

As tensions rose in the East and South China Seas, and the PLA's posture remained focused on Taiwan, some officials and observers have raised the issue of whether it is more urgent to implement the "rebalance" by supporting a forward presence and signaling a sustained commitment to allies. Four Members of the House, led by Representative Randy Forbes, wrote a letter to National Security Advisor Susan Rice in 2013, asking for clear inter-agency guidance to enable a broad effort, to empower departments and agencies to implement that guidance, to communicate to Congress about the required resources, and to convey clarity to U.S. allies and partners. The Members urged the National Security Advisor to lead a review of the strategy on the Asia-Pacific. Although the Members asked for the National Security Advisor to lead an inter-agency review, the State Department responded to Congress. The State Department stated that the Administration laid out its vision for the rebalance, which has sought to strengthen regional institutions, strengthen alliances, support economic institutions, deepen relationships with emerging partners, and build a constructive relationship with China. The State Department asserted that it carries out inter-agency coordination to dedicate more diplomatic, economic, military, public diplomacy, and assistance resources to the Asia-Pacific.[68] On April 28, 2014, Representatives Forbes and Hanabusa introduced **H.R. 4495**, the Asia-Pacific Region Priority Act. The next month, much of H.R. 4495 was included in H.R. 4435, the FY2015 NDAA.

Tension and Trust. Despite the goal of inclusive cooperation throughout the region, there arose competing concerns about the risks of escalating tensions and exacerbating mistrust with China, particularly the suspicious PLA. As the United States and its allies and partners respond to China's military challenges, some are concerned about the security dilemma of a potential

---

[66] Chris Carroll, "Navy Chief: No Big Change in Pacific Force Presence," *Stars and Stripes*, January 11, 2012; Senate and House Armed Services Committees, hearings on FY2013 Defense Authorization, February 14-15, 2012; Tom Donilon, Remarks at the Asia Society, March 11, 2013.

[67] See for example: Senate Foreign Relations Committee, "Rebalancing the Rebalance: Resourcing the U.S. Diplomatic Strategy in the Asia-Pacific Region," a Majority Staff Report, S. Prt. 113–24, April 17, 2014.

[68] Randy Forbes, Rob Wittman, Colleen Hanabusa, and Madeleine Bordallo, letter to Susan Rice, July 23, 2013, and response from Acting Assistant Secretary of State for Legislative Affairs, October 9, 2013. Forbes wrote that the Administration was reluctant to conduct a review ("Stand by Our Ally in Tokyo, *Diplomat*, February 18, 2014).

escalation in hostility and mistrust that could harm cooperation on any common concerns. As Henry Kissinger wrote, "just as Chinese influence in surrounding countries may spur fears of dominance, so efforts to pursue traditional American national interests can be perceived as a form of military encirclement."[69] The PRC's official, authoritative media has defended China's "defensive" policy of "deterrence" and criticized the Air-Sea Battle Concept and other U.S. defense adjustments as directing "Cold War"-like threats against China and provoking China's unspecified "counter-measures." Contrary to U.S. goals in seeking shared interests and access to global commons, some in China have seen an American zero-sum pursuit of "militarism" at the cost of PRC security interests. In contrast to much of the region's welcome of the U.S. presence and concern about China, on November 30, 2011, the PLA's spokesman attacked U.S. announcements about deploying marines to Australia (in an established alliance) and the Air-Sea Battle Concept as "Cold War thinking" and detrimental to regional stability and mutual trust.

On January 9, 2012, the PRC's diplomatic and military spokesmen called the U.S. "rebalancing" strategy's "accusations" against China "groundless" given its "peaceful development." Nonetheless, in March, China announced a 2012 defense budget that increased to $106.4 billion but at a lower rate of growth compared to that in 2011, despite the U.S. strategic shift to Asia. With the announced defense budgets as an indicator, China's rapidly growing economic resources have provided greater funds for what has been already a sustained trend of mostly double-digit percentage increases in real terms since 1997 (after the Taiwan Strait Crisis of 1995-1996).

In June 2012, the PRC defense minister chose not to attend the Shangri-la Dialogue in Singapore to engage with or confront Secretary Panetta and other defense ministers, while the lower-level PLA representative (a lieutenant general from the Academy of Military Science) warned that China should stay calm and not over-react to the U.S. "pivot" to the Pacific. Later that month, the Defense Ministry criticized the U.S. rebalancing strategy as an "eastward shift" in military deployments that counters peace and cooperation. PRC authoritative commentary has depicted the U.S. strategy as directed against China in a bilateral context, though some in China have acknowledged that the U.S. strategy is not simply to counter China.

Some in the United States have advocated attention to accommodation with China to avoid a relationship with a more adversarial, assertive, or aggressive China with rising military power. Such views have included a call for a review of policy of the dispute over Taiwan.[70]

Thus, with a forward presence in Guam and strengthened alliances, U.S. defense has faced the challenges of rebalancing security interests in responding to as well as cooperating with a rising China, while mitigating risks of hostility and planning for crisis management. As the CNO wrote in late 2011, "being forward is critical to deterring aggression without escalation, defusing threats without fanfare, and containing conflict without regional disruption." At the same time, he noted the risk that a country can characterize A2/AD capabilities as defensive and deploy them from its mainland territory, "making attacks against them highly escalatory." The CNO and the Chief of Staff of the Air Force (CSAF) also recognized challenges in the face of budget reductions.[71]

---

[69] Henry Kissinger, "The Future of U.S.-Chinese Relations: Conflict Is a Choice, Not a Necessity," *Foreign Affairs*, March/April 2012.

[70] For example: Michael Swaine, "Avoiding U.S.-China Military Rivalry," *Diplomat*, February 16, 2011; Zbigniew Brzezinski, "Balancing the East, Upgrading the West," *Foreign Affairs*, January/February 2012; Kenneth Lieberthal and Stapleton Roy, "Defuse the Distrust with Beijing," *Washington Post*, February 13, 2012.

[71] Admiral Jonathan Greenert, "Navy 2025: Forward Warfighters," *Proceedings*, December 2011; and Admiral (continued...)

Major Legislation

In July 2006, the Senate Appropriations Committee issued a report (S.Rept. 109-286) on the Military Construction and Veteran Affairs Appropriations Act, which expressed concerns about a construction program on Guam estimated to cost $10.3 billion (with Japan paying 60%) and expectations of a master plan for Guam from the Defense Secretary by December 29, 2006. In the Consolidated Appropriations Act for FY2008 (that became P.L. 110-161 on December 26, 2007), the appropriations committees decided against a Senate provision that would have required the Defense Secretary to submit the master plan by December 29, 2007, and provided more time for a report by September 15, 2008. In response, the Navy Secretary reported on planning for Guam, with initiatives for the Air Force, Army, Navy, and Marine Corps. Also, he reported that the Pentagon was developing the Guam Joint Military Master Plan.[72]

The **National Defense Authorization Act (NDAA) for FY2009** (that became P.L. 110-417 on October 14, 2008) authorized a total of about $180 million for Guam's military construction projects, established a Treasury account for all contributions for military realignment and relocations, and required the Defense Secretary to report on projects by February 15 of each year.

On May 7, 2009, days before Japan's Diet ratified the relocation agreement with the United States, Defense Secretary Gates submitted the proposed defense budget for FY2010. As part of the realignment of the Global Defense Posture, he requested $378 million to start construction in Guam to support the relocation of 8,000 marines from Japan in order to strengthen the U.S.-Japan alliance. This amount would contribute to the total U.S. cost of $4.18 billion for the relocation. The **NDAA for FY2010** (enacted as P.L. 111-84 on October 28, 2009) authorized the first substantial incremental funding for the relocation of marines from Okinawa to Guam, but conditioned upon the Defense Department's submission to Congress of a Guam Master Plan. Among a number of provisions related to Guam in the legislation and conference report, Congress designated the Deputy Secretary of Defense to lead a Guam Executive Council and coordinate interagency efforts related to Guam. Congress also required a report on training, readiness, and movement requirements for Marine Forces Pacific, with a sense of Congress that expansion of Marine Corps training should not impact the implementation of the U.S.-Japan agreement on relocation from Okinawa to Guam. Congress authorized a total amount (including for Defense-wide, Army, Navy, and Air Force) of almost $733 million.

The **NDAA for FY2011** (enacted as P.L. 111-383 on January 7, 2011) changed the name of the Guam Executive Council to Guam Oversight Council. Among the provisions related to defense realignment on Guam, Congress required a report from the Defense Secretary on an assessment of the natural and manmade threats to realigned forces on Guam, the facilities needed to support those forces, and required costs. The House and Senate Armed Services Committees stated concern on December 22, 2010, that the Defense Department failed to report to Congress the detailed plan for projects for the realignment and that the Navy's Record of Decision of September 2010 deferred key decisions, including on training ranges and amphibious landings for the Marine Corps. The committees recommended that Congress defer authorizations for construction for the relocation on Guam pending additional information that includes an updated master plan from the Defense Department. The committees reduced $320 million in the requested

---

(...continued)

Jonathan Greenert and General Mark Welsh, "Breaking the Kill Chain," *Foreign Policy*, May 16, 2013.

[72] Donald Winter, "Department of Defense Planning Efforts for Guam," September 15, 2008.

authorization of appropriations (for three construction projects involving aircraft parking, site preparation, and utilities). The NDAA for FY2011 authorized $176 million for projects on Guam.

On May 26, 2011, the House passed H.R. 1540, the **NDAA for FY2012**, to authorize a total of $303,521,000 for Marine Corps and Air Force projects in Guam in FY2012, after a reduction of $64 million. After Senators Levin, McCain, and Webb called for a re-examination of the realignment of forces, on June 17, the Senate Armed Services Committee completed its markup of the NDAA. According to the committee, it cut about $156 million for two projects for the realignment of Marine Corps forces from Okinawa to Guam because they would not be necessary in FY2012 and the Defense Secretary failed to provide a master plan; and it cut $33 million for grants to purchase items related to the relocation to Guam because the funds would be ahead of need. At the same time, the committee stated that the relocation of marines to Guam remained an important aspect of the U.S.-Japan alliance. The committee reported its NDAA for FY2012 as S. 1253 on June 22. Out of conference, the legislation authorized only $83.6 million for Air Force projects on Guam. On December 12, Guam's Delegate Bordallo expressed opposition to the conference report, for delaying other investments. Enacted on December 31, 2011, as P.L. 112-81, the final legislation also included the Senate's language in Section 2207 on Guam, which stipulated that none of the funds authorized to be appropriated or amounts provided by Japan for projects on land under the Defense Department's jurisdiction may be obligated or expended to implement the realignment of Marine Corps forces to Guam until certain conditions are met. Congress required a force lay-down for PACOM from the Marine Corps Commandant, a master plan for construction from the Defense Secretary, certification of tangible progress on Futenma, a plan on Guam's infrastructure, and an assessment of the U.S. posture in the Asian-Pacific region. (As discussed above, on July 24, 2012, Defense Secretary Panetta submitted to Congress an independent assessment on the U.S. defense posture in PACOM's Area of Responsibility.)

On May 18, 2012, the House passed the **NDAA for FY2013** (H.R. 4310; McKeon) to authorize $229,904,000 for several projects in Guam and repeal the conditions on use of funds for realignment in Guam in P.L. 112-81. On June 4, the Senate Armed Services Committee reported its version (S. 3254; Levin) to continue the prohibition until certain conditions are met. S. 3254 sought to authorize $8,500,000 for Guam (for the Army National Guard at Barrigada) but not the requested projects at Andersen Air Force Base. The final NDAA for FY2013, enacted on January 2, 2013, as **P.L. 112-239**, authorized $159,904,000 for projects in Guam, including $58 million for an unhardened Fuel Maintenance Hangar at Andersen (compared to $128 million for a hardened hangar in H.R. 4310). Related to the realignment of forces in the Pacific, Section 2831 prohibits the establishment of a live fire training range on Guam until the Defense Secretary certifies that there is a requirement for military training and readiness. Section 2832 stipulates that none of the authorized funds and none of the amounts provided by Japan for construction activities on land under the jurisdiction of the Department of Defense may be obligated to implement the realignment of Marine Corps forces from Okinawa to Guam or Hawaii until: (1) the PACOM Commander provides an assessment of the strategic and logistical resources needed to ensure the distributed lay-down of the Marine Corps meets the contingency operations plans; (2) the Secretary of Defense submits master plans for the construction of facilities and infrastructure to execute the lay-down, including a description of the cost and schedule; (3) the Secretary of the Navy submits a plan for proposed investments and schedules to restore facilities and infrastructure at Marine Corps Air Station Futenma; and (4) a plan coordinated by pertinent Federal agencies describing work, costs, and a schedule for completion of construction, improvements, and repairs to the non-military utilities, facilities, and infrastructure, if any, on Guam affected by the realignment of forces. Congress provided exceptions to the restriction on funding, authorizing the Defense Secretary to use funds to complete environmental studies, to start the planning and design of construction projects at Andersen Air Force Base and Andersen South, and to carry out certain military construction projects. Furthermore, Section 1068 requires the Defense Secretary, in consultation with the Chairman of the Joint Chiefs of Staff, to report to Congress, not later than one year after the act's enactment, a review of the strategy, force structure, force modernization plans, infrastructure, budget, and other relevant policies to execute the U.S. force posture in in the Asia-Pacific region (including Guam's operational needs).

The House passed the **NDAA for FY2014** (H.R. 1960) on June 14, seeking to authorize the requested amount of $494,607,000 for Navy and Air Force projects on Guam, modify the amount in P.L. 112-239 from $58 million to $128 million for a hardened hangar at Andersen, and repeal the restrictions on the use of funds in Section 2832 of P.L. 112-239. The Senate Armed Services Committee reported its version (S. 1197) on June 20, which would have authorized $256,334,000 for Navy and Air Force projects and continued the restrictions on the use of funds and Japan's funds for the military realignment, until the conditions are met. As explained by the House and Senate Armed Services Committees on December 10, 2013, the final FY2014 NDAA (H.R. 3304; enacted as **P.L. 113-66** on December 26, 2013) included the House's provision to increase funds to $128 million for the hangar at Andersen, which also would support the 1st Marine Aircraft Wing (MAW) that deploys to Guam for training. The committees also agreed to allow an exception for the use of Japan's funds to construct a utility and a site improvement project, both of which are considered by the Navy to have military value independent of the marines' move to Guam. Section 2822(a) amended the conditions in the restrictions on the use of funds. None of the authorized U.S. funds and Japan's funds may be obligated for the realignment of marines until the Secretary of Defense submits the report required by Section 1068(c) of P.L. 112-239 (on military resources necessary to execute the U.S. force posture strategy in the Asia-Pacific region); master plans for construction of facilities and infrastructure to execute the Marine Corps lay-down in Guam and Hawaii; and a plan coordinated by all pertinent federal agencies on any non-military utilities, facilities, and infrastructure on Guam affected by the realignment of forces. Section 2822(b) provided exceptions to allow the Defense Secretary to use funds for environmental studies and some construction. Section 2822(f) repealed the restrictions in Section 2832 of P.L. 112-239. The FY2014 NDAA authorized the House-approved total of $494,607,000.

On May 22, 2014, the House passed **H.R. 4435** (McKeon), the NDAA for FY2015. As introduced by Delegate Bordallo, Section 1231 requires the Defense Secretary to develop a strategy to implement the strategic rebalance to Asia-Pacific in PACOM's area of responsibility (AOR). That strategy is to be informed by the strategy for rebalancing priorities to Asia as required by Section 7043(a) of the Consolidated Appropriations Act for FY2014 (**P.L. 113-76**) based on language that Representative Forbes introduced. Also based on Bordallo's language, Section 2831 would repeal the restrictions on use of funds for the marines' realignment to Guam in Section 2822(a), the exceptions in Section 2822(b), and the restrictions on development of public infrastructure in Section 2822(c) of the FY2014 NDAA (P.L. 113-66). Section 2831 would insert new language on restrictions on development of public infrastructure. H.R. 4435 would authorize $128,051,000 for Navy and Air Force projects on Guam, including $51 million to establish a MAGTF. Also, H.Rept. 113-446 for H.R. 4435 requires the Secretary of the Army to report by January 31, 2015, on sustained deployment of THAAD missile defense. On June 2, the Senate Armed Services Committee reported its version of the FY2015 NDAA, **S. 2410** (Levin) with Section 2821 to continue the restrictions on use of funds in P.L. 113-66. S. 2410 would authorize $162,451,000 for Guam, $34,400,000 more than the House-approved amount. The $34.4 million would fund a corrosion control and composite repair shop at Andersen Air Force Base.

Author Contact Information

Shirley A. Kan
Specialist in Asian Security Affairs
skan@crs.loc.gov, 7-7606